DRINKING GAMES

AND HOW TO HANDLE THE HANGOVER

Riley King

summersdale

DRINKING GAMES AND HOW TO HANDLE THE HANGOVER

An Hachette UK Company
www.hachette.co.uk

Summersdale Publishers Ltd
Part of Octopus Publishing Group Limited
Carmelite House
50 Victoria Embankment
LONDON
EC4Y 0DZ
UK

www.summersdale.com

Printed and bound in China

ISBN: 978-1-78783-252-7

Substantial discounts on bulk quantities of Summersdale books are available to corporations, professional associations and other organizations. For details contact general enquiries: telephone: +44 (0) 1243 771107 or email: enquiries@summersdale.com.

CONTENTS

INTRODUCTION

What do we have here? Well, genius, the clue was on the cover, but in case you need your hand held, here's a rundown of what's in store.

Part 1 contains those all-important drinking games you're just itching to play. They're sorted into various groupings, depending on whether you're feeling exotic, lazy, lucky or ludicrous.

Part 2 then features a few amusing activities to see how well the alcohol has taken effect. Is that brain of yours still working?

Part 3 is for when the inevitable arrives. It sorts the wheat from the chaff when it comes to hangover advice, and it ends with some ideas of what to fix yourself food-wise to alleviate the awfulness.

Pick, play, enjoy, recover, repeat.

IMPORTANT WARNING

DRINKING EXCESS ALCOHOL CAN DAMAGE YOUR HEALTH.

The publisher urges care and caution in the pursuit of any of the activities represented in this book. This book is intended for use by adults only. The publisher cannot accept any responsibility for the result of the use or misuse of this book or any loss, injury or damage caused thereby.

PART 1

DRINKING GAMES

WHAT'S DRINKING?
A MERE PAUSE FROM
THINKING!

LORD BYRON

WORLD
GAMES

THE
MOST
LIKELY
TO

AMERICA

HOW TO PLAY

YOU WILL NEED:

Three or more players

DIFFICULTY:

You'd better hope your friends think well of you!

Everyone sits in a circle around the room. Going around the circle one at a time, each player asks a "most likely" question. For example, who is most likely to be mistaken for the Queen? Or, who is most likely to be arrested for bad behaviour? On the count of three, everyone points to the person they think best fits the bill. Players take a drink for every person pointing at them. The game continues in this way. Simple but effective!

HOW TO PLAY

YOU WILL NEED:

Three or more players
A variety of alcohol
Shot glasses
An empty glass bottle

DIFFICULTY:

Spin the Bottle for grown-ups!

Place a bottle in the middle of the table so that it is lying down – this will be used as a spinner. Arrange the shot glasses in a circle around the bottle and fill with a range of different drinks. Each player takes it in turn to spin the bottle and must drink whatever it chooses!

SEVEN

CHINA

YOU WILL NEED:
Three or more players

DIFFICULTY:

Do you remember your seven times table?

Start your game of Seven by sitting in a circle. Go around the circle counting but skipping over the number seven – so six goes to eight – because, in China, seven is considered an unlucky number. As the game goes on it gets harder as multiples of seven have to be avoided too – 14, 21, 28 and so on... Every time someone gets it wrong, they must take a drink and the game begins again at one.

CUBAN
JENGA

CUBA

HOW TO PLAY

Two or more players
A set of Jenga blocks
A marker pen

DIFFICULTY: 🥃🥃

Are you Havana good time?

The Cubans love to drink, so get ready to have some real fun! This game involves Jenga blocks, on which you write penalties – or even dares – before starting. For example: "stand on one leg for 30 seconds", "write a 500-word status on Facebook", or "suck an ice cube for one minute". It's just like your usual family game of Jenga, but every time the tower is knocked over the guilty person must take a drink. Every time a block is successfully pulled out of the tower, the player must carry out the instruction written on it or they must finish their drink. Of course, the Cubans play this with shots of rum, or, at the very least, a mojito.

TOPS
TOURNAMENT

SWEDEN

HOW TO PLAY

Three or more players
Cups
A permanent marker
Plastic counters or bottle tops

DIFFICULTY:

Crazy cups!

Use the permanent marker to write all the players' names on the cups, one name per cup. Fill the cups with equal amounts of alcohol and place them in the middle of the floor or on a table – wherever you choose to play. Then gather around the cups in a wide circle, all players an equal distance away from the cups. Go around the circle, taking it in turns to "challenge" one another by throwing a plastic counter or bottle top into someone else's cup. That person must then retaliate by throwing their counter or bottle top into the challenger's cup, and this continues until one of them misses. The person who misses then has to drink the contents of their cup, refill it and challenge another player. If a player throws their counter or bottle top into their own cup they must drink up, refill and try again. If you really want to make things interesting, you can add a nameless cup to the game. Place it in the middle with all the other cups and fill it with a mixture of everyone else's drinks. If someone's top lands in this cup, they have to down the contents!

ALL IS FAIR IN
LOVE AND BEER.

ANONYMOUS

HOW TO PLAY

Three or more players
A large glass
Beer (or other drink of choice)
Vodka

DIFFICULTY: ▮▮▮▯

Beware! Play at your own risk...

To play, fill the glass with your drink of choice.
The Russians traditionally use beer (don't fret,
the vodka comes later!). Stand in a circle and
pass the glass around. Each player must take
a drink and then replace what they have drunk
with the same amount of vodka. Eventually,
the glass will be completely filled with vodka
and the game starts again in reverse, with the
players replacing the vodka that has been
drunk with beer.

HOW TO PLAY

Four or more players

Sonar drinking.

All players sit in a circle. As submarines are underwater, players must do the following: holding both hands stretched out in front of your face, make A-OK signs. Everyone makes a "SHHHH" sound as the submarine dives down, and brings their A-OK signs to their eyes to show that they are now underwater. Now the game may begin.

Each player takes it in turns to say "BOOP" to copy the sounds of a submarine's sonar. One "BOOP" means the game carries on around the circle. When someone says, "BOOP-BOOP" this means the next person must skip a go and stay silent. If someone chooses to mimic the sound of the submarine turning around, "WHOHOO-HOO", then the direction of play changes. Anyone found to be making a mistake must take a drink.

REALITY IS AN
ILLUSION CREATED BY A
LACK OF ALCOHOL.

N. F. SIMPSON

EASY-PEASY PEASY GAMES

YOU WILL NEED:
Two or more players
A clock/watch

DIFFICULTY:

A real no-brainer.

This is possibly the easiest game in the book. Players decide how long (in minutes) the game will last - a recommended duration is five minutes - then each person picks a number from one to twelve. When the second hand of the clock/watch passes a player's chosen number, they take a drink. It's as simple as that!

HOW TO PLAY

YOU WILL NEED:
Two or more players
A TV

DIFFICULTY:

This one won't make your eyes go square, but it may make them a bit fuzzy.

Choose a TV show and invent some rules that dictate when players should drink. For example:

1. Whenever a given character says their catchphrase, take a drink

2. Whenever you see a scene in a pub, take a drink

3. Whenever you see a certain item of clothing, hair colour, accessory, animal – take a drink!

VODKA
ROULETTE

HOW TO PLAY

YOU WILL NEED:

Two or more players
Vodka (or any other clear spirit)
Shot glasses
Water

DIFFICULTY:

Are you feeling lucky?

Fill as many shot glasses as there are players with water, except for one, which should be filled with vodka (or your other clear spirit). Mix up the glasses and hand out the shots. Everyone must down their shot at the same time. Whoever gets the vodka (the person with an unhappy look on their face and probably demanding a glass of water!) loses and is out of the next round. Repeat until there is one player left: they are the winner and can choose a drinking penalty for the other players.

HOW TO PLAY

YOU WILL NEED:

Two or more players
A bag of peanuts

DIFFICULTY:

Not recommended for people with a nut allergy or for those who are fussy about having salty bar snacks unceremoniously plopped into their drink!

Each player drops a peanut into their own full glass at exactly the same time when someone shouts "Drop!" The peanut will sink to the bottom, then rise up again. The player whose peanut comes to the surface last is the loser and must drink their entire glass. The loser's glass is then refilled and another round is played. After each round, players must retrieve the peanut from their glass, eat it and take another one.

Three or more players

🍺

No secret password required.

This one is best played on a pub crawl, while walking between pubs, but you can have a go at home if you're not too precious about your furniture! The rules are simple: if someone shouts "Tree house!" everyone must get themselves (both feet) off the ground, e.g. up onto a step, a bench, a wall or, if you're feeling adventurous, a tree. The last person to do so must buy the next round or, if you're playing at home, down their drink.

For a sillier twist, why not change the trigger word or even make it a phrase such as "I like turtles!" or "Rubber baby buggy bumpers!"

I ONLY TAKE A DRINK
ON TWO OCCASIONS:
WHEN I'M THIRSTY AND
WHEN I'M NOT.

BRENDAN BEHAN

CARD
GAMES

HOW TO PLAY

Three or more players
An empty pint glass
A pack of cards

DIFFICULTY:

Prepare to feel the burn!

All players must sit in a circle, with the empty pint glass in the centre. Make the "Ring of Fire" by spreading the cards face down around the glass. Players then take it in turns to select a card and follow these instructions:

Ace is for waterfall – drink from when the person to your right starts drinking and stop drinking as soon as they stop drinking.

2 is for you – choose someone to take a drink.

3 is for me – you drink.

4 is for floor – last person to touch the floor drinks.

5 is for guys – men drink.

6 is for chicks – women drink.

7 is for heaven – last person to point to the sky drinks.

8 is for mate – you pick a person to drink with you every time you have to. The rule is passed on when another player picks up an eight.

9 is for rhyme – you say a word and each player around the circle must say a word that rhymes with it. The first player to hesitate or make a mistake must drink.

10 is for thumbs – you must place your thumb discreetly on the table at some point; the last player to do likewise must take a drink.

HOW TO PLAY

Jack means make a rule – this can be anything from no first names to no swearing; if a player breaks the rule they must drink. Rules are rescinded when a new rule is made (or continued if you're up for it).

Queen means make a toast – everyone drinks "to the Queen".

King is for King's Cup – pour the remainder of your drink into the pint glass.

The player who picks up the fourth and final King must pour the remainder of their drink into the pint glass, get up onto the table, cry "I'm king of the world!", then down the drink.

HOW TO PLAY

YOU WILL NEED:
Two to four players
A pack of cards

DIFFICULTY:

Pony up and prepare to do some drinkin'!

Remove the aces from the pack and then lay five to ten cards face down in a row, end to end (the more cards, the longer the game) – this is the "racing track". Place the aces (your respective "horses") in a row perpendicular to (but one card space below) the track to create a broken "L" shape.

Players must then name the "horse" that they think will win, and bet a number of fingers of their drink on the horse – the more you bet, the more you can dole out for other players to drink. Things can get pretty heated in the world of gambling, so make a note of everyone's bets at the start of the game! When all bets have been raised, the dealer takes the rest of the pack and turns over the top card. Whichever suit the card is, the ace of the same suit is moved forward one place along the track. The dealer continues in this manner until one horse wins the race by reaching the last card of the track.

The winner gets to dole out the fingers "in the pot" to any one (or a combination) of the other players.

I'D RATHER HAVE A BOTTLE IN FRONT OF ME THAN A FRONTAL LOBOTOMY.

DOROTHY PARKER

HOW TO PLAY

YOU WILL NEED:

Two or more players
A pack of cards

DIFFICULTY:

Hook, line and drinker.

Each player is dealt five cards and the rest of the pack is roughly spread out in the centre. The aim of the game is to make pairs, though if any players have pairs in their hand from the start they must discard them and take replacement cards from the pack.

Player one begins by choosing a card in their hand and asking another player of their choice if they have any cards of that rank. If the player in question has any card that matches the value of the one requested, they must give it to player one and drink two fingers of their drink if it's a numbered card, or three fingers if it's a picture card or an ace. Player one may then place the pair face-up in front of them and take another

turn. If player two does not have any card of the requested rank, they reply "Go Fish" and player one must drink a finger of their drink and pick up another card from the centre. (If the card they select makes a pair with one in their hand, they may discard the pair, but play still passes to the next player.)

Whenever a pair is laid down, all the other players must drink two fingers of their drinks. Play continues clockwise until one player gets rid of all their cards. The winner is the player who has discarded the highest number of pairs when the game ends – they can choose a suitable forfeit for the losers.

A MAN'S GOT TO
BELIEVE IN SOMETHING.
I BELIEVE I'LL HAVE
ANOTHER BEER.

W. C. FIELDS

ACROSS
THE
BRIDGE

HOW TO PLAY

YOU WILL NEED:
Two or more players
A pack of cards

DIFFICULTY: ■■■

It's safe to drink on this construction site.

Deal ten cards face down in a row, side by side, to form the "bridge". Players take turns to flip over a card; if they reveal a numbered card, they're safe and play passes to the next player. If they turn over a picture card or an ace, they must drink a finger of their drink and add more cards to the bridge, depending on the card they turn over:

Jack – one finger, one card
Queen – two fingers, two cards
King – three fingers, three cards
Ace – four fingers, four cards

The game ends when all the cards on the bridge have been turned, or the pack runs out.

BEAT
THE
DEALER

HOW TO PLAY

Three or more players
A pack of cards

DIFFICULTY: ▉▉▉

Beat the dealer with your card skills, not your shoe.

First, decide if aces are high or low, then cut the cards to decide who will be the dealer. The dealer holds the deck and the player to their right tries to guess the numerical value of the card on top. Without revealing it, the dealer looks at the card and tells the player whether they are right or, if not, whether it is higher or lower than their guess. The player is allowed one more attempt before the card is revealed.

The player must then drink the number of fingers' difference between their guess and the card's value. So, if the player's final guess was five and the card was an ace (low), they must drink four fingers.

If the player guesses the card correctly on their first turn, the dealer must drink six fingers; if they guess right on their second turn, the dealer only has to drink three. Once three players have had a turn, the role of dealer passes to the next player clockwise.

The used cards are placed face up in numerical order, so that all players can see them. As more cards go out, it gets easier for players to guess correctly and beat the dealer.

ALCOHOL, TAKEN IN
SUFFICIENT QUANTITIES,
MAY PRODUCE ALL
THE EFFECTS OF
DRUNKENNESS.

OSCAR WILDE

HOW TO PLAY

YOU WILL NEED:

Three or more players

Spoons (one less than the number of players)

A pack of cards

DIFFICULTY: ▮▮

Does not involve any intimate cuddling.

Players sit in a circle with the spoons in the centre, handles facing outwards and spoon ends touching. For each player in the game, you need four cards of the same rank from the deck. For example, with four players you could use the aces, 2s, 3s and 4s. The cards are then shuffled and four are dealt to each player. The aim of the game is to collect four of a kind.

Everyone looks at their cards, selects a card to discard and places it face down to their left, picking up the discarded card from the player on their right. This continues throughout the game.

HOW TO PLAY

Once a player has four of a kind they can take a spoon from the centre and then resume playing as before, but always discarding the card they have just picked up so that they keep their set of four.

The person who doesn't manage to grab a spoon loses and must down their drink and sit out the next round. Play starts again with one less set of four cards and one less spoon and continues until only one spoon remains – the player who ends up with this is the winner.

GAMES
OF
CHANCE

NASTY
OR
NICE

HOW TO PLAY

YOU WILL NEED:
Two or more players
A coin

DIFFICULTY:

This game is only half sugar and spice.

This is guaranteed to get everyone in the party spirit, and is best played in a bar that has a good shots menu, or at home with a selection of spirits.

Order a variety of shots from the bar (or, if you are at home, pour some out). Make sure that there is at least one shot per person, and that about half of them are shots that taste "nice" (think sweet ones such as Irish cream, spiced rum, peach schnapps) and the other half are "nasty" (think tequila, black sambuca, absinthe). Each player takes it in turns to flip the coin, guessing whether it will land heads or tails up. If they get it right, they get to drink a shot of their choice. If they get it wrong, the other players choose for them – it's up to them to choose whether a "nasty" or "nice" shot is in order!

HOW TO PLAY

YOU WILL NEED:

Two or more players
A die
Six plastic cups
A marker pen
A jug

DIFFICULTY:

Roll up! Roll up! It's time get your drink on.

Take the plastic cups, number them one to six on their side with the marker and set them out in a row on a table. Fill the jug with an alcoholic beverage of your choice.

Players take turns to roll the die; when a player rolls a number which corresponds with an empty cup, they can fill it with as much drink as they like. Play then passes to the next person. If the cup they roll already has some drink in it, they must down the contents and then roll again. Remember when you're pouring drink into a cup that you could well be the person who ends up drinking from it!

HOW TO PLAY

YOU WILL NEED:

Two or more players

Two dice

DIFFICULTY:

Six is the magic number.

This game is simple but effective if you have a large amount of alcohol to work your way through. Players take it in turns to roll the dice; if the numbers add up to six (for example, a four and a two) or one of them is a six, the player must drink one finger. If a player rolls a double, they must drink fingers equivalent to the number on one of the die – so if they roll a double four, they must drink four fingers. For a double three or double six, both rules apply: a finger for adding up to six, and a number of fingers for the double. So a double six means eight fingers: two for two sixes, plus another six for rolling a double six!

HOW TO PLAY

YOU WILL NEED:
Two or more players
A plastic cup
Two dice

DIFFICULTY:

Aye chihuahua!

Players take it in turns to shake the two dice in the cup and slam them down on the table. Without letting anyone else see, the player takes a peek at what they've rolled and announces their score. Rather than adding the dice to get a score, the two numbers are combined with the highest always coming first: for example, a three and a two would make 32, a five and a four, 54, etc. A two and a one, 21, is known as a "Mexicali" and beats all other combinations.

The aim is for each roll to be higher than the last person's; if it isn't, then players must bluff. When a player is accused of bluffing they must reveal the dice: if they were lying they must take a drink, but if they were telling the truth, the accuser must drink. If a player is caught bluffing a Mexicali, they must down their drink.

Try adding your own rules, for example:

A **61** means everyone must take a drink.
A **31** means the play changes direction.

ALCOHOL IS A
MISUNDERSTOOD
VITAMIN.

P. G. WODEHOUSE

HOW TO PLAY

YOU WILL NEED:
Three or more players
A coin
An empty glass

DIFFICULTY:

Test your nerve and your drinking mettle.

Players sit in a circle with the empty glass in the centre. Player one takes the coin and the person to their right must pour some booze into the empty glass – the more reckless they feel, the more drink they will pour into the glass. The player doing the pouring then calls "heads" or "tails". Player one must then flip the coin: if the other player has called correctly, they take the coin and play moves on, with the person to their right now adding to what's already in the glass. If they have called wrongly they must drain the glass in the centre, and player one takes another turn at flipping the coin.

SOMETIMES TOO MUCH TO DRINK IS BARELY ENOUGH.

MARK TWAIN

VERBAL GAMES

THE
CELEBRITY
GAME

HOW TO PLAY

Two or more players

DIFFICULTY:

This game will give you stars in your eyes.

Players should gather around a table or sit in a circle. Player one turns to the person on their left and says the name of a celebrity; the next player then has to think of a celebrity whose name begins with the first letter of that famous person's surname, e.g. if the first celebrity named is Chris Evans, the next one could be Ed Sheeran, and the next could be Sophie Turner, and so on. This continues around the table; the direction will be reversed if someone says a name where the first letter of both the first name and the surname are the same, e.g. Marilyn Monroe. The most important rule is that you must play this game without pausing. If you do pause you have to "drink while you think", drinking continuously until you think of a person.

HOW TO PLAY

YOU WILL NEED:
Three or more players

DIFFICULTY:

Time to own up.

Players take it in turns to name something that they have never done; for example, "I've never eaten a whole Toblerone in one sitting." If any of the other players have done this thing (honesty is key, of course!), they must take a drink. With this game you can play to your advantage by saying things that you know the other players have done.

If any of the other players think that you are lying, they may say so and if they are right, you have to down your drink. If they are wrong the joke's on them and they have to finish their own drink!

DOWN
AT THE
ZOO

HOW TO PLAY

YOU WILL NEED:

Three or more players

DIFFICULTY:

Do not feed the animals.

Each player must choose an animal they would like to be during the game, and an action to go with it. Before play begins everyone announces their animal and demonstrates their action – for example, if they choose to be a lion they might roar and claw the air with one hand. The sillier you make your action the better. The first player does their animal action followed by that of any other player they choose. Play then passes to that player, who must do the animal action of the first player, their own action, and the action of another player, and so on. Play continues until someone makes a mistake and has to down their drink, or until your sides are hurting from laughing so hard at each other doing awful animal impressions.

SLAP,
CLAP,
CLICK

HOW TO PLAY

Two or more players

Get into the groove. Or not.

This is one of the hardest games to play – those without a good sense of rhythm will be in trouble! Before starting the game a category has to be decided, such as "animals" or "film titles". Players sit in a circle or around a table and begin the game by slapping their thighs with both hands simultaneously, then clapping their hands together and finally clicking their fingers with their left and then right hand. This routine should build up into a steady four-beat rhythm that goes: slap, clap, click, click.

Whilst the players are doing this they have to take turns to call out a word belonging to the category decided, keeping strictly to the rhythm by saying the word on the fourth beat, at the same time as the final click of their fingers. If a player fails to think of a word when the beat gets to them – or they lose the rhythm or say a word that doesn't fit the category – they must take a drink. Play continues until everyone's arms get tired.

NOW IS THE TIME
FOR DRINKING, NOW
THE TIME TO DANCE
FOOTLOOSE UPON
THE EARTH.

HORACE

HOW TO PLAY

YOU WILL NEED:

Two or more players
Sticky notes
A pen or pencil

DIFFICULTY: 🍺🍺

This is one instance where intense confusion occurs way before the hangover.

One player should write down the name of a famous person on a sticky note and stick it to the forehead of another player.

Everyone can see the name on the note except the person on whose forehead it is stuck. This person must find out who they are by asking questions to each player in turn. Only "yes" or "no" may be given as answers. For every "no" given the guessing player must take a drink. Once the first player has determined who they are, play moves on. Continue until everyone's forehead is thoroughly sticky.

HOW TO PLAY

Two or more players

Can you string one together?

Someone starts with a word – any word will do. The next person has to say a word that could help make a sentence with the word that has just been said, and so on. For example: the first person may say "Elephants", the next may say "like", the next "peanuts", etc. The game goes on until someone says a word that doesn't make sense, or until someone hesitates, or until they laugh so much that they can't talk. This person then has to take a drink and the game continues. The sentences constructed when this game is played can become absolutely bizarre (and hilarious), especially if some of the players are lateral thinkers, but as long as the sentence makes grammatical sense, it will count.

HOW TO PLAY

YOU WILL NEED:
Three or more players

DIFFICULTY:

Fuzzy duck? Duzzy...

Players should sit in a circle. The first player turns to their left and says, "Fuzzy Duck"; the next person turns to their left and does the same. This continues until a player turns to the person who's just said "Fuzzy Duck" to them, and says "Duzzy?" The question changes the direction and the phrase to be repeated then changes to "Ducky Fuzz". Anyone can reverse the direction by saying "Duzzy?", but each person may only do it twice per round.

The idea is to go around the circle as fast as you can; stalling or getting it wrong means you have to take a drink. It's probably best not to play this one within earshot of your mother-in-law/local priest/young children.

I'M NOT A HEAVY DRINKER; I CAN SOMETIMES GO FOR HOURS WITHOUT TOUCHING A DROP.

NOËL COWARD

SILLY GAMES

UNDER-
WATER
KARAOKE

YOU WILL NEED:
Three or more players

DIFFICULTY:

Check check one two one two.

Each player takes it in turn to perform a song for their "audience". The catch is that songs cannot be sung – they must be gargled through alcoholic beverages! The other players try to identify the song being "sung", and each incorrect guess is punished by a drinking penalty. If, after a second gargled rendition, none of the players can guess the tune, the performer must finish their drink.

Continue for as many rounds as your ears can bear!

HOW TO PLAY

YOU WILL NEED:

Three or more players
A stereo

DIFFICULTY:

Musos and boozos unite!

One player is nominated as the DJ and the others take turns to identify songs being played. The DJ plays only the first five seconds of the track before stopping it. If a song is incorrectly guessed after the allotted time, the player must down their drink; if a song is correctly guessed, play moves to the next person.

A player can guess in less than five seconds, subject to the following drinking penalties/ bonuses if they get it wrong/right:

1. A wrong guess at four seconds – player drinks four fingers; a right guess – DJ drinks one finger.

2. A wrong guess at three seconds – player drinks three fingers; a right guess – DJ drinks two fingers.

3. A wrong guess at two seconds – player drinks two fingers; a right guess – DJ drinks three fingers.

4. A wrong guess at one second – player drinks one finger; a right guess – DJ drinks four fingers!

Continue until the DJ's start/stop-track finger gets sore.

ALCOHOL MAY BE
MAN'S WORST ENEMY,
BUT THE BIBLE SAYS
LOVE YOUR ENEMY.

FRANK SINATRA

FOLLOW
MY
LEAD

YOU WILL NEED:

Three or more players

DIFFICULTY:

The blind leading the blind.

This is a copycat game, but instead of a "Simon says…" instruction, players must deduce by observation the action they must copy. Any player may choose to do an action at any time. For example: someone might decide to put their thumb on their forehead, and everyone has to follow suit. The last person to catch on has to take a drink.

HOW TO PLAY

YOU WILL NEED:

Three or more players
Twister
Four types of alcohol

DIFFICULTY:

Put your flexibility to the test!

This game is identical to a regular game of Twister except that the play is made even harder by the introduction of alcohol. Assign a different type of alcohol to each coloured circle, for example, blue could be beer. Spin the Twister dial, and when the person places their hand or foot on the circle they must also be fed a shot by the person in charge of the spinner. If a person falls they must take two shots as punishment.

HOW TO PLAY

YOU WILL NEED:

Two or more people
A timer or a digital watch
Cups or shot glasses
Beer

DIFFICULTY:

The ultimate stamina test!

This game can be played with any number of people. Line up several shots of beer for each person playing, and drink a shot every minute for 100 minutes (refill the glass after every hit). Set a timer or simply pay attention to a clock with a second hand. You can have this game running in the background while you chat or watch TV, or you can try reciting tongue twisters at top speed or dancing around between shots to spice things up. The person who lasts the longest is the winner. Make sure each shot is small – the key to winning here is pacing.

HOW TO PLAY

YOU WILL NEED:
An even number of players (four or more)
A long table
Plastic cups

DIFFICULTY:

Scull your way to drunken victory.

Be warned: things can get really messy with this game! Divide into two teams and line up on opposite sides of a long table. Each player will need a cup filled with drink – make sure the cups are all the same size and filled to the top.

On the count of three, the first player on each team starts to drink. Once they've drained their cup, they slam it upside down onto the table, which is the signal for the next player in their team to start drinking. If a player spills any of their drink, or turns their cup over before completely finishing it, their cup is refilled and they have to start again. The same goes for any overly keen player who starts drinking prematurely when the player before them hasn't yet finished.

The winning team is the first to have all its members finish drinking. They may then choose a forfeit or drinking penalty for the losing team.

I DISTRUST CAMELS,
AND ANYONE ELSE
WHO CAN GO A WEEK
WITHOUT A DRINK.

JOE E. LEWIS

HOW TO PLAY

YOU WILL NEED:
Three or more players
A stereo
A note (paper money)

DIFFICULTY:

Easy money.

This game is similar to Pass the Parcel, but requires much less preparation. Everyone sits in a circle except for the DJ, who is responsible for playing and stopping the music. Players must pass a note around the circle; whoever is holding the note when the music stops must take a drink. If two people are touching it, mid-exchange, they must both drink. Play continues until a person has had the note stop at them three times – they are the winner and may also claim the note as their prize!

Four players
Two ping-pong balls
Twenty plastic pint glasses
A long(ish) table
A "side drink"

DIFFICULTY: ▊▊▊▊

Prepare to get batted!

Set out the pint glasses in two sets of ten, in a triangular 4-3-2-1 formation at each end of the table, and fill them all at least half full with beer.

Players divide into two teams and position themselves at opposite ends of the table. A player from each team takes their turn to throw their ping-pong ball into any one of the glasses at the end opposite to where they are standing.

Every time a team member scores, a member of the opposite team must drink the contents of the cup the ball has landed in. The aim is to eliminate all of your opponents' cups first. If any player misses the cups completely, i.e. the ball lands on the table or on the floor, they must take a drink from their "side drink".

To spice things up a bit, have a few "killer" cups in each set, containing something like whiskey, vodka or rum.

BUT I'M NOT SO
THINK AS YOU
DRUNK I AM.

J. C. SQUIRE

THE
AFTER-
DINNER
MINT
GAME

HOW TO PLAY

YOU WILL NEED:

Two or more players
A pack of after-dinner mints
   (the flat, wafer-thin kind)
Shot glasses

DIFFICULTY:

The perfect digestif?

Each player takes an after-dinner mint and pours themselves a shot of alcohol. At the word "Go!" players must place their after-dinner mint on their forehead and, with their hands behind their back, attempt to get it into their mouth without touching it at all.

If a player drops their mint, they must down their shot. Play continues until you get sick of the taste of booze and minty chocolate.

THE
SINKING
SHIP

HOW TO PLAY

YOU WILL NEED:

Two or more players
A pitcher of beer
An empty glass (not too heavy!)

DIFFICULTY:

Man the lifeboats!

This nerve-racking game will have you holding your breath as the tension mounts: be prepared to get covered in booze at some point!

Each player should have their own full glass of drink at the beginning of the game. Sit around a table, with the semi-full pitcher in the centre. Put the empty glass, upright, into the pitcher so that it floats. You may need to pour a small amount of drink into the bottom of the glass before play commences to give it some stability. Each player then takes it in turn to pour some of their own drink into the floating glass, waiting a few seconds to see whether or not the glass sinks. Play continues in this manner until the glass finally does sink. The unlucky player who causes this to happen must fish the glass out from the bottom of the pitcher and down its contents.

PART 2

HOW DRUNK ARE YOU?

TEST ONE

While you are still relatively sober, familiarize yourself with the stages of drunkenness you are likely to experience during the night:

CONFIDENCE: ☐ YES ☐ NO

Getting louder is a sure sign you are on your way to drunkdom. Go on, have another one…

DANCE WALKING: ☐ YES ☐ NO

Wanting to dance instead of walk to your intended destination is a sure sign of alcohol taking over, but remember, from here on it's a slippery slope between getting merrier and just getting more pissed.

ASSERTIVENESS: ☐ YES ☐ NO

Becoming more vocal with your opinions and confiding to strangers that you'd give the PM a run for their money is one sign that you are switching from a happy drunk to a raging lunatic. Advice is to lay off the vodka for a while.

GETTING WEIRD: ☐ YES ☐ NO

Meeting new people and immediately expressing your love for them is a big indication that you have passed the tipsy stage and are fast approaching stalker mode. Did anyone tell you that doing this is really NOT cool?

NEAR PARALYSIS: ☐ YES ☐ NO

If you're stumbling around in the vain attempt to dance while you still have smears of dried sick around your mouth, then take yourself to bed (or ask a responsible adult to carry you there).

TEST TWO

BLURRED VISION – HOW CLEARLY CAN YOU SEE?

Decipher each letter and unjumble them to make a word describing your state:

TEST THREE

THE SEARCHWORD – IS YOUR BRAIN STILL FUNCTIONING?

Find the following words in the puzzle below and prove yourself sober, or not:

BLADDERED

TIPSY

SLOSHED

LEGLESS

BLOTTO

X	A	N	N	Z	L	O	K	Z	C
S	E	S	L	O	S	H	E	D	H
C	V	Q	T	V	M	X	C	N	N
B	L	A	D	D	E	R	E	D	T
N	E	X	T	U	L	X	G	Z	I
N	G	Y	I	A	X	D	E	Y	P
K	L	D	X	Q	B	C	H	U	S
D	E	K	X	U	E	B	M	O	Y
G	S	I	H	L	P	W	W	G	Z
H	S	V	B	L	O	T	T	O	A

TEST FOUR

DRUNKEN DOT-TO-DOT – TEST YOUR HAND–EYE COORDINATION

Focus your mind and complete the following dot-to-dots. (If you're feeling hardcore, try spinning round three times before you start.)

37• 36• •35

38• •34

39• •33

40• •32

31•
30• •20 •19
•21 22• 23• •18
41• •24
29• 25• •17
28• 26• •16
42• 12• 27• 15• •16
13• 14• 9•
43• 11• 10• •8
44• 7•
45• 5• 6• 3•
4• •2
46•
47• 48• 49• 1•
50•

22• 21•
23• 20•
24• 13• 14• 15• 16• 17• 19•18•
12• 11• •8
10• 9•

•25 •7

•26 •6

27• •5
1• 2• 3• 4•

129

I WILL NEVER
DRINK AGAIN

PART 3

HOW TO HANDLE THE HANGOVER

HANGOVER TRUTHS AND MYTHS

You've heard of the "hair of the dog" hangover cure, right? Well, I tried it after a rather unrestrained night on the bourbon and I'm *still* coughing up my pup Rowdy's fur. Don't risk it! I've suffered so you don't have to. My friend Sanch said you're actually meant to drink *more* alcohol the day after, but Sanch is not to be trusted after the pipe incident. That's all I'll say about that. Anyway, I feel it's now my duty to debunk some of the other myths that are floating around out there, and to confirm some actual good advice. Here goes…

LIQUOR TO BEER – NEVER FEAR

MYTH

Although there is some truth in this, it's got nothing to do with what's different about the ingredients of these different types of alcohol. In fact, it's really down to the volume of the drink and how much you consume. For instance, if you start off drinking singles with a mixer and follow with pints of beer, you'll drink less of the latter, as it's a heavier drink and more likely to make you feel bloated, meaning that your intake slows down.

H$_2$O, ALCOHOL, H$_2$O, ALCOHOL

TRUE

When you've gone to the bar for a few drinks, the main thing on your mind is alcohol. But if you know it's going to be a heavy night, drinking water in between your "real" drinks will help reduce (but not cure) your hangover symptoms. You may not get as wasted as you usually do, but you'll certainly feel better for it in the morning.

WINE IS FINE

MYTH

Certain wines, especially red, contain a large amount of tannins and sulphites, which are known to cause headaches. But there is a glimmer of hope for the winos out there, as sulphite-free wine is available in most supermarkets, although it's slightly more expensive than your average sulphite-loaded wine. Whiskies and other malt drinks are also bad for headache hangovers. Drinks that are known to be gentler are beer and clear liquor.

WOMEN AND MEN SUFFER THE SAME

MYTH

Those women who like to drink their male friends/partner under the table will probably still be under the table the next day while the man is out and about. Because women store more fat in their bodies, which doesn't absorb alcohol, this means more alcohol flows through their bloodstream, making them feel more drunk that night and more hungover the next day.

HONEY WILL MAKE YOU FEEL SUNNY – AND LEMONS TOO

TRUE

Studies suggest that honey is good for hangovers because it contains fructose, which helps speed up the breakdown of the alcohol. Lemon is said to be conducive to the recovery time as it has alkaline properties which help restore balanced pH levels in the body. So while you're having a pint of water the day after, try adding some honey or a slice of lemon to it.

COFFEE WILL MAKE YOU FEEL DANDY

MYTH

When you wake up, bleary-eyed, and reach for the kettle, think again before you have your dose of coffee, or anything with lots of caffeine in for that matter. If consumed in relatively large amounts, it makes you even more dehydrated and could end up making you feel worse. Instead, if you want something hot, try herbal tea as it is known to relieve nausea and is packed with antioxidants, vitamins and minerals.

PAINKILLERS FOR PREVENTION

MYTH

Popping pills when you're drunk isn't good for anything and won't make your hangover subside the next day as the effects will have worn off by then. Instead, take a couple of aspirins in the morning, an hour before you need to start functioning.

SLEEP TIGHT IN DAYLIGHT

TRUE

Sleeping specifically when it's daytime won't help cure a hangover but sleeping as much as possible will help make you feel better. Although we tend to "crash" when we've had too much to drink, our actual sleep is disrupted by our body's attempt at breaking down the alcohol. You are permitted to have as many power naps the next day as you like!

ONE MORE DRINK
AND I'LL BE UNDER
THE HOST.

MAE WEST

SWEAT IT OUT IN THE SAUNA

MYTH

You might think sweating the alcohol out through your skin is a quick fix to cure a hangover but think again as it could potentially be very dangerous. Because you're already very dehydrated your body will go into shock as you quickly launch yourself into extremely sweaty conditions. As well as this, it can damage blood vessels and disrupt your normal blood flow.

SWEAT IT OUT DOING EXERCISE

TRUE

Exercise is good for a hangover if done in moderation and at the right time. As your body will feel fragile, don't go setting your alarm for 7 a.m. to get in that early morning 10 k, but do try going for a brisk walk or leisurely bike ride (that's if you're not still over the limit) after lots of water and some food. The fresh air will do wonders, too.

HANGOVER RECIPES

NO-STRESS FARM HOUSE FRY-UP

THIS ONE IS GOOD IF YOU DON'T WANT MUCH WASHING-UP.

SERVES 3

INGREDIENTS

4 tsp olive oil
300 g sliced, parboiled potatoes
250 g sliced mushrooms
100 g spinach, torn
3 eggs

Optional
Paprika
Baguette, torn into pieces
Parmesan or Cheddar cheese, grated

1. Warm 2 tsp oil in a pan, add the potatoes and sauté for 4-5 minutes over a medium heat, until browned.

2. Remove from heat and decant potatoes into a bowl.

3. Add another 2 tsp oil to the pan along with the mushrooms and place the pan with the lid on over a medium heat for 5 minutes. Remove lid, turn up the heat and fry until the mushrooms are browned and there is no liquid.

4. Put the potatoes back in and add the spinach, sauté for 3 minutes, then break in 3 eggs. Replace lid and cook until the eggs have just set.

5. Season with a sprinkle of paprika and top with the pieces of baguette, if you like, and serve with the Parmesan or Cheddar.

FRENCH TOAST

THIS IS A GREAT QUICK AND EASY CURE.
TRY TOPPING IT WITH SLICED BANANAS,
CHOCOLATE SAUCE, MAPLE SYRUP OR
STRAWBERRY JAM.

SERVES 2

INGREDIENTS
4 eggs
1 cup of milk
1 tsp of sugar
1 tsp of salt
Butter
Slices of bread without the crusts

1. Beat the eggs and the milk together and add the sugar and salt.

2. Heat a knob of butter in a frying pan. Dip a slice of bread in the egg mixture and then heat slowly for a couple of minutes on each side until golden brown.

3. Serve hot with your choice of toppings.

PROTEIN-PACKED PASTA

IF YOU'VE MISSED BREAKFAST, THIS WILL GIVE YOU AN ENERGY BOOST.

SERVES 2

INGREDIENTS

3 tbsp olive oil
2 chicken breasts, diced
3 rashers bacon, chopped
1 garlic clove, crushed
Salt and freshly ground black pepper
150 ml double cream
250 g farfalle

To serve
100 g Cheddar or Parmesan cheese, grated
Handful fresh basil, torn

1. Heat the oil in a frying pan, add the chicken and bacon and cook on a medium-high heat until the chicken is golden-brown and cooked through.

2. Add the garlic and cook for 1 minute. Season with salt and freshly ground black pepper, then add the cream and keep on a low heat.

3. While frying the chicken and bacon, cook the pasta according to packet instructions in a pan of salted boiling water, then drain.

4. Add the creamy chicken and bacon mixture to the cooked, drained pasta and stir well.

5. Serve and garnish with cheese and basil.

SUPER-DETOX SMOOTHIE

YES, IT MIGHT BE GREEN AND, YES, IT MIGHT NOT LOOK DISSIMILAR TO WHAT HAS ALREADY COME UP THIS MORNING, BUT THIS SMOOTHIE WILL HELP YOU RECOVER FROM THE DEADLIEST OF HANGOVERS.

SERVES 2

INGREDIENTS

1 cup mixed berries, frozen
½ cup pineapple, papaya or mango, diced
1 cup dandelion greens
½ cup spinach
½ cup coconut milk
1–1½ cup coconut water

1. Place all the ingredients into a blender.

2. Blend until mixed thoroughly.

3. Pour into a glass and drink slowly, so you savour the taste and your body can absorb the nutrients.

CHICKEN NOODLES

NUTRITIOUS, WHOLESOME AND HEARTY FOOD – JUST WHAT IS NEEDED FOR A HANGOVER.

SERVES 2

INGREDIENTS

1 tbsp olive oil
4 chicken breasts, diced
1 garlic clove, crushed or sliced
1 red pepper, thinly sliced
1 green pepper, thinly sliced
5 spring onions, sliced
100 g bean sprouts
2 × 150 g packs dry noodles
3 tbsp oyster sauce

1. Heat the oil in a large frying pan, then stir-fry the chicken until golden and cooked all the way through.

2. Mix in the garlic and peppers and cook for 2 minutes. Add the spring onions, bean sprouts, noodles, sauce and 5 tbsp water and stir-fry everything for another 2 minutes. Serve immediately.

BEANS ON TOAST

A CLASSIC RECIPE WITH A TWIST.

SERVES 2

INGREDIENTS

2 eggs

4 slices of bread (fresh is best)

1 tbsp olive oil

1 onion, diced

½ tsp ground cumin

½ tsp ground coriander

85 g semi-dried tomatoes from a jar, chopped if large

400 g can baked beans

Butter, for spreading (optional)

To serve

Fresh coriander or parsley, chopped

Ground cumin

1. Bring water to the boil in a saucepan for the eggs. Heat the oil in a frying pan, then add the onion and gently cook for a few minutes until it starts to brown. Mix the spices into the pan and stir briefly. Add the tomatoes and beans and cook until warmed through.

2. Turn down the heat under the saucepan so the water is just simmering, then crack in the eggs and gently poach them until the whites are firm but the yolks are still runny. Toast the bread, then layer the beans onto the toast (buttered or unbuttered, as you wish) and place the eggs on top.

3. Serve with a sprinkle of extra cumin and coriander or parsley.

DELICIOUSLY SMOOTH SMOOTHIE

IF YOU'RE PUT OFF BY HOW HEALTHY THE SUPER-DETOX SMOOTHIE SOUNDS (ALTHOUGH IT TASTES AMAZING), TRY THIS INSTEAD.

SERVES 1

INGREDIENTS

1 whole large ripe banana

1½ cup milk

2 tbsp honey

1. Place all three ingredients into a blender.

2. Blend until smooth.

3. Pour into a glass and raise a glass to getting rid of your hangover.

CONCLUSION

There you have it. That's your lot, dudes. I've given you all the games, activities, wisdom and culinary secrets I've got. Now it's over to you. Get out there and have fun. Share in the hilarity, pass on the advice, cook up a cure.

My lawyers have told me I have to remind you (again) to drink responsibly and not die while playing the games (or making the recipes, lol) because then there'll be hell to pay, and Riley King ain't got that kind of cash. Stay safe out there... please!

If you're interested in finding out more about our books, find us on Facebook at **Summersdale Publishers** and follow us on Twitter at **@Summersdale**.

www.summersdale.com

Image credits